The Bottle Episode

CL Bledsoe

Poems in this collection appeared in the following places in similar or sometimes much worse forms:

"2020" appeared in *Tipton Poetry Journal*, who nominated it for a Pushcart Prize.

"Albatross Soufflé" and "Bird Home" appeared in *Bending Genres*

"August" appeared in *Pine Hills Review*

"Bad Luck" appeared in *Change Seven*

"Baskin Robbins," "Noisy Neighbor," "Wake Up," and "Things I'm Going To Do When I Can Do Things, in No Particular Order:" appeared in *Alien Buddha Press*

"But the Sun, Also, Is a Liar" and "Brain as an Unwound Clock" appeared in *Last Leaves*

"The Distance" appeared in *Oddball Magazine*

"Dogwoods" appeared in *Inquietudes Literary Journal*

"Highway 284" appeared in *Whimperbang*

"A Honeysuckle Vine" and "Writing Spider" appeared in *Bourgeon*

"How to Find Joy" appeared in *Maryland Literary Review*

"Keep Looking" appeared in *Cajun Mutt Press*

"A List of Side Effects" appeared in *Feral*

"A Mail Order Class On Entropy" appeared in *On Loan from the Cosmos*

"Moon Dust" appeared in *Poetry Poetics Pleasure Zine*

"Probably Named Jim, "This Is How I Heal," and "To Know Thyself" appeared in *Ponder Savant*

"A Sigh Made of Misspent Choices" appeared in *Trouvaille Review*

"Strange As Angels" appeared in *Zoomoozophone Review*

"Victory in Japan Day" appeared in *NoVA Bards*

"When I Was a Boy" appeared in *A Farther Room Press* and *Pif*

"Whoops" appeared in *A Farther Room Press*

"A Yelp Review of Life" appeared in *Academy of the Heart and Mind*

"You Can Never Go Home Again, Even if You Find the Key" appeared in *MockingHeart Review* and *A Farther Room Press*

"We Must Tell Our Sons" appeared in *Poetry Quarterly*

Contents

The Distance 7

Lenny Bruce Is Maybe a Little Afraid 8

How To Find Joy 9

Victory in Japan Day 11

Strange As Angels 12

Albatross Soufflé 13

Bird Home 15

A Sigh Made of Misspent Choices 16

August 17

But the Sun, Also, Is a Liar 18

Brain as an Unwound Clock 19

List of Modernized Southern Writing Metaphors 21

Honeysuckle Vine 22

Writing Spider 23

When I Was a Boy 24

Highway 284 25

The Cow Graveyard 26

Mamaw's Chickens 28

Feeding the Fish as the Sun Rose 29

My Brother, Laughing 30

My Sister, Before We Got Old 31

The Chittering Leaves of Morning 32

Some folks say there ain't no bears in Arkansas 33

She Asks Me about My Family 35

Recurring Dreams of My Hometown, after Christopher Fullerton 37

Raspberries 38

This Is How I Heal. 39

To Know Thyself 41

Probably Named Jim 43

A Mail-Order Class On Entropy 44

Whoops 45

Bad Luck 47
Moon Dust 48
Dogwoods 49
A List of Side Effects 51
2020 53
Baskin Robbins 54
Noisy Neighbor 55
Things I'm Going To Do When I Can Do Things,
in No Particular Order: 56
Keep Looking. 57
Confession 58
Planting Peas 59
Trade your body for a silent room, flattened by faces 61
Watching X-Files in the Dark with You 62
When We Lived On the Sun, We Wore Different Shoes 63
We Both Know We're Not Getting Out Alive 64
Last Train to Dubuque 65
The sweetened breath of the starving. 66
A Yelp Review of Life 68
The Flying Children Tell Their Story 69
The Miracle 71
The Sun 72
The Ghost Nebula 73
Mom Was a Tropical Frozen Drink 74
A Lovely Shade of Purple 76
The Weight 77
Dinner Time 78
The Flowers 80
How To Slay the Dragon 82
Marrying the Storm 83
We Must Tell Our Sons 85
Magic Death 86
You Can Never Go Home Again, Even if You Find the Key 88

The Distance

If you stare long enough into
the distance, you won't notice
the wind unlacing and stealing
your shoes. All of us are busy
making mistakes we can blame
on somebody else. If you don't
like what I said, whose fault is
it? The problem is continuing
to trust that this is the worst
things can get, when the evidence
is pretty clear. Drive as far as
you can and then remember
gas exists. If you can convince
enough people, you can launch
a car into space and call it science.
Who do you think will insure it?
They think of the moon as a man
because it's pale, cold, and distant.
These days, we don't even bother
naming our gods. That's why
they never get our prayers.

Lenny Bruce Is Maybe a Little Afraid

My zucchini wouldn't grow so I picked
it. Two more took its place. When we logged
into the virtual meet-and-greet for her class,
my daughter told me that she told the kid
who won't stop talking about his chickens
that she had a fake ear, and he never sat
by her again. I texted her mom and she said
"Jesus, we did good." The teacher was careful
to talk in terms of when they would meet
in person again, not if, but none of the students
would turn on their cameras. My plan before
my body fell apart was to have my credit card
paid off before the election, to lose weight,
to get healthy. Who knows where the riots
will lead. I doubt freedom. But I want to believe
in hope.

How To Find Joy

Start in the last place you looked.
Beneath the dusty couch pillow
some dead aunt gave you one

holiday. Under the dampening
trash bag in the kitchen that doesn't
smell bad enough to take out. Yet.

Put your ear to the wall and whistle
softly to see if anything answers.
Hope nothing does. This is also

a good way to tell if a stampede
is coming. You may have to move
to a new apartment. Put your tongue

to the door when no one is around.
You're looking for something
between almonds and safe. Everyone

knows what you mean, but no
one can spell it on the first try. It's
okay. The trick is never to let

the punitive patter of regret memorize
your apartment number. When it asks,
give it the president's cell, your fourth

grade teacher's bottled disdain, a perfect
afternoon six years from now. It doesn't
matter. As soon as you make eye contact,

it's going to duck into a rattling elevator
and pray that it doesn't fall too fast.
If it's still on its feet at the bottom,

it's doing better than most of us.

Victory in Japan Day

The look in your eyes, the way you hold me
with their sadness – we're married, like in old

movies no one watches, grandmother waiting
for a dead man to return from the war, his face,

a box of delicate letters. Nights, holding hands
as the fire dies, quiet except for the sparks. A song

playing in some other room. Time creaking out
in an old rocker. A new name for beauty to distract

from the dying. The circle of your eyes is the ring,
worried on a finger when you're not near. All of this

has been said before, but darling, I'm home from
the war. It's Victory in Japan Day. We won. We won.

Strange As Angels

There's a chicken roasting in the oven
with potatoes the way you like them,
asparagus on the clean stove. Candles, blues,
and beer. This is my offering to tempt
you home; please understand: voices rise
outside the window—everyone thinks
it's Tuesday—and nothing helps
except your smell in your closet
while you're at work. That's where my desk
went. I'm sorry I told you it was stolen.
I was overtired from keeping the drafts out.
All day, murderers come to the door trying
to sell cookies, but I'm on a diet. When
the electricity shoots from your eyes, the blood
flower exploding to engulf the ceiling, take
my hand. I have a place we can hide.

Albatross Soufflé

There's no secret to how the world is made:
it isn't. It grows from the leavings of holy
box turtles, flightless origamis, snufflings
lost behind elder doors. Tears and Tvarscki,
Chopin and Coffins. My daughter's goodbyes
that settle into my heart and never ease out.
It's okay if you don't believe me; I'm a notorious
liar who is probably just trying to get into
someone's pants. Probably, honestly, my
own, which seem to have shrunk. I'm not
saying you aren't as special as you think
you are, but I'm not not saying that. We're
all the villains in our own stories looking
for a hero to defeat us before we destroy
it all. The world was left here by a nerdy
scientist who fell in love with a cloud shaped
like his father. Hair cuttings swept into a dustpan
and forgotten after the comets came. A bad
idea with little planning. This explains most
but not all things. Such as what my neighbors
are doing that sounds like a pile driver?
An advertisement for paprika-infused
albatross. A list of shrubs all grown from
the forgotten plans of the person you were
supposed to save. If I were to say I ache like
a horse smelling the grass beyond the fence,
a nesting bird dreaming of the sky, something
I can't name but would gladly trade for store
credit, would you believe me? What if I

complimented you and your mother? Let's
pretend we know what any of this means
long enough to fool the rubes. It's probably
all the clouds' fault; they take in as much
as they can, until they become real, and then
they have to let some things go. It's a lesson
in impermanence for all of us.

Bird Home

Let them settle in me, a phone line
drooping between tree corpses,
chatter somewhere above my ears
that smells of spices I can't name.
I don't mind choking on feathers
if it makes something in me rise,
a lightness in the stomach, a dark
calm in the throat. I'm not
the kind of person who throws rocks
at placid waters, anymore. I like to watch
as they fly with the seasons. Only
I can hollow these clunky bones,
climb up somewhere worth jumping
from. And when I jump, it's on me
to forget to fall. I'd rather cheer
on the starlings than envy the crows.
It's a choice to start singing: hey you,
passing in the wind, come rest
beside me for a little while.

A Sigh Made of Misspent Choices

A dumber bird never crashed
into clear glass, my heart,
long shed of feathers, a dead
thing's milk, shoved too far
back into the fridge, sour
and frozen. It's never going
to be of use. It's taken almost
as long to realize that as it has
to grow the thing. Plain as death,
it lingered too long on the lines
wind forms in dust, thinking
they were words. It skitters
when it should prance, cowers
most days, and never perks up
when its name is called. Throw
a stone any way, and some
smarter heart will sue. Formed
of fat and cloudstuff, unable
in its best year to see the creases
in its toes. I wish I could say
it's biding, waiting on a phone
call, planning something
worthwhile, but the mountain
rumble roar belies the truth. All
I ever asked was that some soft
hand smudge the glass. Even
this is too much, I know.

August

It always smells like August, fish
dying on a shore too far away to hear.
I wanted to tell you they found something
wrong in my brain, but I forgot you'd died.
That's sort of what they found. How does
anyone sleep here? All of us are murderers
and none of us have anything worth stealing,
which is a kind of détente, I guess. But what
happens when one of us needs to keep
in practice? Someone's been calling me
at home every Thursday. She doesn't see
how broken she is because she doesn't
know what shards look like. I'm not going
to be her glue, anymore; bodies don't fit
together that way. I'm sorry they lied about
that. Every time I talk about back home, I learn
that something I believed was a lie. This
is why I don't ask after you anymore. But
I miss believing in you.

But the Sun, Also, Is a Liar

With the day-old donuts, you can start
to feel like the concrete forgives us
our trespasses. The same with the used
shoes, still smelling of animal and something
that's forgotten what animal is. Who
the hell can afford to live? Wandering
the thrift store is like vacationing
in someone else's life. Were these things
once precious? Was I? So many hours
spent to buy trash. Like everyone,
I was seventeen once and knew more
than time ever could, all of it golden
guesswork that would later prove to be
right. But it doesn't matter. Someone's
always going to hurt better than you,
which doesn't mean you can ever give up
on trying. Children should always be
dirty and smiling or you've done something
wrong. I remember one afternoon, my uncle
shooed me out from under my father's feet,
in the Fish Shack, where they teetered,
drinking and hating each other. He told me
to go play outside. That's what kids were
supposed to do, not cling in fear to their father's
clinging in fear while their mothers were
dying on the hill far above. I sat in the dirt
until my shoulders, legs, and neck burned.
There was something important he meant
me to learn.

Brain as an Unwound Clock

Some kid playing screaming
music downstairs. Lean in close
so I can tell you what I think of you
as soon as I think of something
about you. The way that a cup
responds to tea, over time, this
is the way thoughts are coated
by hatred, negative impulses.
This is not to say that forgiveness
isn't a fool's errand. Rather,
I knew a speed freak who said
he liked to wake up to a new
world every fifteen minutes or
so. If you were to ask me how
I feel, I would first have to stare
at the ocean for nearly an hour –
not too long but just long enough –
sometime after the sun has begun
to set, sand cooling, spray on skin.
Or, the flow of traffic on the street
shimmering in the sun as I walk
back to my desk from the psychiatrist
I don't trust who wants to put me
on lithium. I've always liked the song,
but the trees, shading my way make it
an easy ten, fifteen degrees cooler.
It's nice outside as long as you're
inside under air-conditioning. I don't
like to think of this as the hottest

summer in the last 100 years; I like
to think of it as the coolest summer
of the next 100 years. While old
white men drive by in convertibles.
A kind of ambivalence, I suppose.

List of Modernized Southern Writing Metaphors

Watering the dying cypress trees, representative of virtue signaling.
A well-meaning but impotent preacher as commentary on sealioning the conversation about affordable mental health options.
Painting a crumbling capitol building, representing the death of unionization.
Tooth decay as a metaphor for class mobility.
Something strange but unspoken about a thicket, as a metaphor for women's rights.
A drunken old man who falls but doesn't realize he's hurt, representative of creeping voter disenfranchisement.
Sharing a recipe for an inedible dessert as a metaphor for American exceptionalism.
An orphan child who is never named, representative of violence against the LGBTQ community.
The Misfit as metaphor for #alllivesmatter.

Honeysuckle Vine

A honeysuckle vine grew down
the ditch wall, choking the bracken
in the corner below the road. We'd

clamber up the debris and washoff
to pick the flowers, taste the drop
of sweet, more taunt than meal,

then slide our muddy jeans down
to the bottom. Sucking steps took
us over to the road, to play in the pipe

that ran under. If you were tall
enough, you could walk it, hands on
one wall, feet on the other. They

told us it was dangerous, what if
it collapsed under the weight
of traffic? When they tried to send

us home or to school over the bridge,
we said but you said it's too
dangerous, what if the road collapses?

Writing Spider

It was black with yellow stripes,
or maybe the other way around,
in a big web by the overgrown

back door we were scared of.
The legend was that if you spelled
out a word in stones nearby, it

would copy it into its web. Hence
the story about the needy pig,
though I always preferred the rat.

We started with Fuck. When
that didn't take, Shit. Maybe
this was a puritanical spider,

so we tried Butt. Inside, the living
room was quiet because Mom
was dying in her bed. The light

faded until Dad dragged in,
slurring his steps and bitching
about the lack of dinner. After

we peeled potatoes and put them
on to fry, I snuck out in the cool
of the porchlight and spelled Help.

When I Was a Boy

I stood in the rain many times, but I never
turned into a fish. Mouth open to catch
the warm drops, I swore I could hear
the ocean when I put my ear to the bank.
But it was just mud crying to be a man.
Never let it trick you into taking its hand.
Once it leads you to the loam world, where
everything is soft and despair is too stove
up to chase you with its belt, you'll never
want to come back. Swimming through
the thick soup of air with no particular
place to go. When the fog came,
I'd stand on the levee and call my father's
name, but he never opened the bridge.
It was just me and the mudcats flopping
down below, the dumpgulls gorging.
They say in the big city, somebody steals
the rain before it hits the ground. We drove
through Memphis on the way to the hospital
where they told me my brain was broken.
It hasn't rained since then, not really.

Highway 284

Old truck bodies exploded
in the soybeans. Dirt tracks
sizzling. So many dogs that
aren't sleeping. Beside
the cemetery we used to pretend
wasn't just old rocks and grass
over the long dead—and we
weren't just eying the door but
afraid to bolt—a peach orchard
whose owner might shoot you,
the ground littered with rotting
fruit. Bowlegged boys they say
will grow out of it. Girls already
learning to keep quiet. There
is never-ending war, here. Weeds
have just as much right to the soil.
The roads arc long and strange,
following some dead rich man's
land. Trailers creep into the fields.
The sky, alive with dragonflies,
feasting on mosquitoes. Your
leg will husk over in an afternoon.

The Cow Graveyard

Bleached bones scattered among
sun-burned Bermuda grass, switch-
grass, bitterweed. We followed
the trail – dragged by whoknows –
behind the lake, the gravel hills, all
of them picked clean except the wind,
which still carried the ghosts of meat,

past the devil's walking stick,
which was just thorns – how dumb
the devil must be – until the hills valleyed
against the back of the Frankenstein
place – a joke we never made, for
some reason. There, the grass thickened
with black shards, whole spines,

tufts of hair, and magic. We were quiet,
there, in case something was listening.
The ground was littered with puzzle
pieces with missing edges; not even
the devil could put them back together.
Nestled in the hills, we couldn't hear
cars, trains, mom screaming her weird

pain out when the dementia got too
bad. All we could hear was the myth
of the brother and sister, abandoned

by their parents, who went into the woods.
If they ever came back out, it was as
something changed and hard, different,
something that couldn't be hurt.

Mamaw's Chickens

The chickens couldn't get to the roof.
But they wanted to. They could only

fly up a few feet. They'd start on
a stump or a car, something fairly low,

then glide across to the rusty swing
set for the grandkids who'd all grown

up. From there, a short tree. They
were pretty far from the building,

now, but they'd launch themselves
at it, glide to the door, and work their way

up. I must've been the only one who saw
them doing it. I told Dad and he said simply

chickens can't fly. I didn't have the words
to explain: sometimes, you don't need to.

Feeding the Fish as the Sun Rose

More grayish-brown than blue,
agitators stirred up the water to
mix it with oxygen in a rainbow

spray. Early, before the sun found
our names, we'd skim its surface
in an old boat that seemed as much

patch as aluminum. Pushed out
from the shore by a Mercury's still
spinning blades, Dad wouldn't let

me hold the fish feed bag. I imagined
we were motoring toward some
secret place. Charybdis, calmed,

behind me, or transformed into Charon
to guide me to the shore. There'd
be something there I couldn't even

explain, maybe there weren't words
for it yet, or maybe just no one
had taught them to me.

My Brother, Laughing

I wonder if he laughs like that
now that he's found Jesus.

Supplicant's throat
cocked back soft.

Is the world still a horrorshow
shocked into joy for the briefest
moment?

I've found him, too. The things
my brother used to laugh at, mostly
he'd now consider sinful. He did
then, too. That's why he laughed.

My Sister, Before We Got Old

You were lightning
distracting from the thunder.

The Chittering Leaves of Morning

Maybe if the sky would shut its dumb
face for a minute, I could enjoy this snack
cake. I don't think it's too much to ask
that the patterned world shift to make space
for whatever I'm in the mood for. Trees
and things are pretty, but have you ever
seen TV? Cartoons? There are vitamins
for sunlight and injections, if all else fails.
Air comes in aluminum cans. Somebody
can dig those out of the trash and make
a buck. There is literally nothing that
couldn't benefit from a coat of paint,
depending on the hue. Sure, cars can be
ugly but have you ever seen an armadillo?
A mole? Some of them don't even wear
clothes. I've seen them. On TV. Make a big
fire and throw all the real into it. Roast
marshmallows—or better yet, get s'mores
ready made out of a package. You'd adjust
in a week. If you didn't, there are pills.
You think you're so special you deserve
a discreet experience with reality? At best,
you're living a discount rack life. Coupons
and duty free. It's fine. All of it's fine. Relax.

Some folks say there ain't no bears in Arkansas

-after a line by Lyle Lovett

Another way of explaining struggle is a list
of instructions on how to get a bear
into a boat in order to cross the Mississippi

before anyone finds out. Recognize that
you're going to get wet, best case
scenario. There are two primary methods

that've been investigated in the literature. First,
place a large jar of honey and/or salmon into
the boat. Hide, somewhere, downwind. (You

now smell like honey or salmon. Remember
that for later.) Then, simply wait. The other
involves appealing to the bear's better nature,

i.e. trying to confuse it with academic jargon
relating to philosophy but mostly drowned
in your own preconceptions based on class

privilege, so that it climbs into the boat to get
away from you. Once the bear is in, you'll realize
you haven't considered how you'll get in,

yourself. Ask it politely if it knows a good
place to get a drink around here, but don't try
any obvious lines. If the bear's ears prick up,

it probably can hear the assassins. Honestly,
this is a good distraction. The thing about bears
in boats is they don't so much steer as try

their best to roar down the wind. It's your turn
to listen as the bear explains why you should've
taken 64 East. Even West Memphis is better than this.

She Asks Me about My Family

Begin with mud, the long-wet kind you've got
to keep clomping through so you don't sink
right in—where do you think fertilizer comes from?
          it's not just the hopes and dreams sloughed
          off. There's people in there, also, people
          too slow to keep ahead of the threshers.
          They say that's where we came from.
The wildflowers were all eaten by cattle, but the bitter
weeds dot the pasture with yellow. If you want out
you better gather all of them, weave them
into a rope, and find somewhere to hang it.
The only way out is down. It's not so much
a question of opportunity as of selecting
the appropriate rage. Is it the deep fire
orange or the dull blood? Which goes best
with your aesthetic? Your personal brand?
Watch out for cow shit. It's everywhere.
A shovel. My father's shovel. My brother's shovel.
Uncles' shovels. My shovel.
To lift the landscape and peek underneath.
My mother hiding from the sun in a room that's
bright in a different way.
The grass is an ocean and I nearly drowned.
Sorrow isn't the only thing sucked into the mud.
Fall, the smell of cut grass. Ashes in the breeze.
This is a kind of love, but that doesn't make it right.
Mud tracked into floorboards, laundry room, steps long ago
covered with it wiped from boots.
A corpse, patted out and left beside the road.

None of us knew each other's names. It was Boy,
Doing Good, the Mayor of Worthless.
Windows rolled down by hand to move the heat around.
Fingers running on levees as we ease past.
I was never one of them, but I wanted to be.
Dad came to us when I was fifteen, after mom
was gone and said there wasn't nothing for me, here.
Fence posts strung with barbed wire, tufts
of cow fur where they'd scratched.
Trucks whose bumpers had fallen off, cut in half, welded into
something new for the hell of it.
We were so poor we didn't know what poor was.
I never figured out who left all those designs in the asphalt.
Maybe it was the sun, bored.
Everything lost itself after too long out in the heat.
Chickens spending all day getting from the ground to the roof,
only to come back down and start again tomorrow.
I never understood the rage, the bowed heads.
Angry ain't the same as safe.
I remember some nights, waking, the earth shaking.
I lay still, but it never swallowed me.

Recurring Dreams of My Hometown, after Christopher Fullerton

After the war, the library is the only
survivor. It simply had more bullets
than the churches, whose coffers ran
dry once they moved Sunday night
football to 8 a.m. Cows roam
the mostly deserted streets, looking
for someone to milk. Skin tone
determines type of milk—chocolate,
2%, skim. None of us is whole.
The dead rise from the funeral home
to get the crops planted, lie down
in the ditch and wait for harvest time.
I would like to say I have a purpose,
as I walk the streets, hiding from
the sound of bells. I'm looking for
someone I've always known. Her
name is just around the next corner.

Raspberries

Sometimes, you need a professional opinion
to know you're alive. Something in writing
that says, "Not yet!" A laminated piece

of paper of indeterminate size that you can
flash in the dumb and mean faces of the world
to say, "Ptthhbbbbttttt!!" For at least long

enough to let you catch your breath. Respect
would be too much to ask. Empathy or
consideration—let's be serious. Everyone

is barking at their own mailman who is clearly
coming to murder the only person who knows how
to work the can opener. Everyone misses their

mother, or what she should have been. What I'm
saying is go for the knees. They're the structural
flaw that will bring the whole thing down.

This Is How I Heal.

I wash enough things
to make me forget
my hands. I count

dogwood blossoms
until I've forgotten
how many times

I've started over.
I make a video in
the stairwell I just

cried in trying to
sell it to the French.
Offer the squirrels

outside the window
nuts until they pancake
on the glass. Then feel

strangely ashamed. Some
people who don't
understand time think

it exists all at once.
The past is now.
The present is the past.

And the future is
something that happens
to other people, who

were better at planning
or just had more luck
than I ever did.

To Know Thyself

Start with the proper accoutrements:
a bowtie with soft colors. A hawk's
wing draped across your clavicle.

Look at what the pretty people do
and then don't do that. If you don't
know what to wear, I know a guy

who knows a guy. What I'm saying
is it's good to have friends, even
if you have to pay for them. Who

do you think isn't collecting a check
from you? When the villagers come,
slip a mustache onto your upper

lip and tell them the bastard ran out
the back not five minutes ago. Grab
a pitchfork and a torch. Hope

to God that mustache glue holds.
They make it from the neediest horses,
so. The thing is, you weren't meant

for any of this. No one was. You
were supposed to be a dancer or
lie on the couch for three weeks

straight or find someone who sees
the you you forgot to make yourself
The one that's clever and cool. Someone

who somehow isn't disappointed
in the you you became instead because
of traffic and poor time management.

Good luck. There's not a one of us who
wouldn't settle for a nice dessert and
something to talk about that isn't ourselves.

Probably Named Jim

Whoever came up with life
insurance was a genius or
a sucker. The value of dissolute

minerals, the odd carved shell
weighed against the shareholders'
faith. I am at my best when

I'm recycled, a worm's timeshare
he dreams of retiring to someday.
Everything you die for is

a long-established lie, except
Chocodiles, which exist
as part of a publicly traded

entity. Find me an ounce of love,
justice, quiet. There is a kind
of machinery, oiled with the sweat

and blood of somebody else. It grinds
ever onward while we all try
to pretend we're not screaming.

Remember, as a child, how you
thought nothing? And then,
the first time you realized what

they'd made for you, you raged?

A Mail-Order Class On Entropy

Now that I'm not dying as specifically,
I get to bed earlier each night and wake
earlier each morning. Another hour
recovered; eventually, I'll get my childhood
back. I may not know how to be loved,
but I know how to be ignored and still keep
the kitchen clean. Who was the first person
to see a bee, playing in flowers, and think –
I bet their children eat really well. Same
with the cows. With the chickens, we cut
out the middle man. This is how we learned
to eat our own young, who don't taste as
good, it's true. If you wait long enough
in one place, someone will come. Maybe
love, probably the cops. It could well be
both, or rather, you'll learn to appreciate
the comforts of the cuffs. At least someone
cares enough to bother with you, even
if that means locking you in a cell. Sometimes,
the only way to put something down you've
carried too long is to set it on fire and walk
away.

Whoops

The door closed quick like a finger
through the pudding of the morning.
I don't think I want to lick it clean.
The taste of regret, sagging from
my ears. A greasy slime exuding
from fingertips. I want you to come
into my arms and whisper recipes
for chocolate cake while I smell
your hair. It's not my fault the roads
were closed every time I tried to get
back to Topeka. The door didn't close;
it was closed, and now I can't get
back in unless I'm willing to knock
softly or possibly ring the doorbell.
But there's no one there to answer.
A welcome mat that asks for your phone
number. A gold knob of regret. I took
out all the curbs so you couldn't kick
me to one, and now the pizza guy
doesn't know where to park. Don't
think I won't eat it in the street. Please
let me back into my own apartment
or throw me down the stairs and tell me
your middle name. Mine is Jehoshaphat.
Or I wish it was. Someday, someone
will look past everything I've done
and see what I could do with a little
encouragement and a cattle prod. Girl,
I heard you like books. I have so many

in my gray head. Let me whisper them
into your ear while I make you a cup
of tea and a scone. That's all I ask. That,
and the sex.

Bad Luck

It's hard not to envision seams,
when the rain slides the same
way each time, the wind bends

around blankness not even cats
notice. The eye fixes on pattern,
and finding none, forces it.

People kill each other to decide
whether to name it or bow
in shame. Which cloud's heart

did I neglect? Or was it my cells
in a previous incarnation who
never called the sun back after

a lovely night of drinks? To say
there's no hand on the back
of my neck would be comforting

if it weren't for the chafe
of the palm, the labored breath
I hear just behind my ear.

Moon Dust

You learned love from the moon's attentions
           to the sea. When light strikes,
it leaves fire and pain, rot replaces vibrancy.
           Best to sing from a distance
and hope you aren't heard. When they learn
           someone has survived, they'll
do their best to eat you in hopes of tasting
           regret. Hire the greatest
marketing firm known to America,
           and you won't change
a single heart. (Also, keep an eye on your
           vintage tie collection.)
Hatred is a waste of time, but that doesn't
           mean you should ever trust
those who carry ketchup in their chest
           pockets. If they get too close,
show your teeth. You've spent a lot
           to reveal the bone in them.

Dogwoods

Every evening, the dogwood branches, shifting
outside the window, a susurrus of voices on the edge
of memory. Every evening, our hero waits
for the light against the clouds. The light from.
Every evening, he keeps it to himself, about the way light
falls into the dirt, and from that, they say, something
can be born—but only if there's someone to catch it. He's trying

to be the dirt and be someone. Do you really think
the people who tried to wed you to the camera
and the audience vote can be trusted to give directions
anywhere worth going? Death, my friends,
is the greatest fertilizer. Try to stop snickering
and read that again. Listen, I'm never coming
to your party. I'm too busy trying not to die to compliment

you on your kitchen. Come over here, and we can hold
hands until I remember what hands are for. Probably,
you don't get what you want from me, and I don't get
what I want from you. This is as close
to fair as life gets. Maybe you're just not used to being part
of something larger than yourself, like
a major extinction event. If it helps, I get so nervous

sometimes, I swallow my cup so I don't have to ask
where the recycling is. This is how the world
ends: it's belly full of plastic, dumb eyes reflecting
pain, which means we're at the forefront
of fashion. We've had thousands of years to make

something of the world, and we never
even learned its name. We could ask forgiveness, but forgiveness

is like light; someone has to be there to catch it. Maybe
the hero gets up from that chair. Maybe the darkness
has brought its warmth, and he wants to microwave something
to help with the headache. Maybe, this is all
there is, flowers caressing the window glass. Who sent them?
            Maybe he should go out and see.

A List of Side Effects

You may confuse a spider's hunger
for affection, an understanding
of economic principles. Biological
imperatives once relegated to
the trash might flare up at 2 a.m.
when you're trying to sleep,
reminding you, "Psst, you're
going to die alone and the whole
thing makes everyone sad when
they think about you." Bloating
after gorging. A desire to return
to those halcyon days that never
actually existed. You will listen
to the same song over and over
and then wonder why your brain
doesn't work anymore. May include
bursts of anger at trivial things,
like the guy in the breakroom who
poured water out of the tea pot
so it would boil quicker and then
didn't refill it when he was done,
people not zeroing out the microwaves
so the next person has to do it, people
who don't rinse the sinks after
they use them. Pretty much anything
breakroom related. Your back
will itch in hard-to-reach places
and no one will help you except
the corner. You won't stub your

toes on the way to the bathroom
at night, but you will forget to take
that file back to work for three days
straight. Inertia in the evenings.
A manic exhaustion like ants on
cocaine are eating your brain. A
desire to stop, throw it all away,
and go back to the cave you
wasted so many lives in. But don't.

2020

Weren't there worse times
than this? My father side-eyed
a world war that claimed his
brother, drank his way across
Japan. My uncle was on the wrong
side of history in Little Rock, stood
over a mountain of Korean skulls
in a photo Mamaw hid in the attic,
but they assured us Jesus forgave
him on his death bed. These
are just the horrors I know. Ancient
tree limbs grooved. Bodies kept
from the river. Time isn't so much
a cycle as a wheel, grinding
to a stop. Once it shakes us off,
it will probably roll smoother.

Baskin Robbins

It wasn't long ago an itching in the ear
meant death, which is fine as long as
everyone can go out for ice cream, after.
My neighbors have been stoned since
the birth of their baby, who I suppose
has been stoned, too. I can smell it
in everything, the little death to tide
them over. Nothing is anyone's fault
unless they choose it to be, which is
another way of saying free will, which
falls away with a complex enough
investigation. I'm not supposed to say
I understand what it is to be away,
to wish to be away from every moment.
Bourbon is cheaper than a casket. These
days, weed grows in the streets. You
can see the cracks in the sidewalk
where it's poked through.

Noisy Neighbor

When the bastard kept bumping up against
my windows, I flung the door open, went
around the side of the house, and told
the night I was going to kick its ass. Some
of us have jobs in the morning, I said, fists
in close approximation of small balls, ears
already red. It didn't have anything to say
to that, let me tell you. Just who do you think
you are, buster? I asked. And did it have
anything to say? All night, I'd been sitting
there, minding my own, while this jerk used
up all the light, made a mess of things—you
couldn't even see the ground for all its sprawl.
We have to share this place, I said. I'm a
reasonable man. You just go away and never
come back and I won't call the authorities.
It's up to you, I said. I'm clearing off my
schedule. I gave it a good, fierce glare
and waited for any response. When there wasn't
any, I nodded, proud, and went back inside.
I slept like a babe, let me tell you. When
I opened my eyes in the morning, it was gone.

Things I'm Going To Do When I Can Do Things, in No Particular Order:

-Get a tattoo of Tattoo from Fantasy Island, probably not on my face.

-Train a squirrel to vacuum in a little French maid's costume.

-Start going to the fancier Dollar Tree that's a little farther away.

-Buy all those funny tee shirts I'm always seeing advertised, then sweat in them a bunch and sell them to fetishists.

-Travel...to the couch to watch TV.

-Buy a new set of tires...and set them on fire right outside the door of my neighbor's apartment the next time they play music too loud.

-Maybe buy some new socks.

-Invest in sex robots, which are clearly the future.

-Finally watch *Gilmore Girls*.

-Find happiness and contentment...probably on my couch.

Keep Looking.

Plant flowers whose faces
you forget in the night. Arrange
towels artfully as though
they've never been used. Something
has to feed the dark. I've made
a list of ways not to die. First,
say my name the way you did before
you knew me. Second, make
another list. When the sink stops
dripping, find something else
to fix. The secret to living
forever is to never remember
where you left death. Probably
stuck it in the freezer again.
Or maybe it's been on top
of your head this whole time.

Confession

The way to cure sadness is to light
a candle, face the wind, and complain
about the wax blowing in your face.

Crystals probably help, as long as
you don't ask where they came from.
Dirt dyed gold. A celebrity endorsement.

Everyone in this town is so busy
celebrating themselves, they haven't
noticed the flames rising up the curtains.

But who would dare deny them
their fireworks? Heaven is just another
country club, and I never learned

to play golf. I was always so dumb,
I preferred walking through the grass,
building guillotines with the caddies.

At night, the flames help us see
where to place the blade just right.

Planting Peas

You used to know how to do this—one
imagines memory lives in the bones
and not the belly—stab three inches
down with the blade that disemboweled
the ghost that lives in your attic, down
below the loam. Stare meaningfully
until you and the seed are both super
uncomfortable and then laugh—a real
rolling-belly, open-mouth guffaw, like
when you were sixteen talking shit with
your friends and never again since. Just
one, unless you want to give it root rot
or unrealistic expectations of joy. Whisper
your hopes for the coming weeks into
the soil so that the seeds nestle in among
them before they become failures. Hope
devoured tastes sweetest. Cover the seed,
the hope, the laugh with the soil you stole
from the old lady in the building across
the parking lot, the one with all the plants
you used to watch and watch until you
saw she goes to bed at 8:30, so you climbed
up onto her balcony and took the slightest
clump of perfect soil. You emptied your
pockets and shoes into the hole and smoothed
it over. She will never know. Maybe she'll
even compliment you on your peas once
they grow. You'll feel like shit but take it.
Turn your head to the side so that your ear

covers the buried seed and let pour all dream
juice rattling around in there. Not too much—
Most of what's in your head is dream—you
don't want to drown it. Don't worry that
the seeds might be dead since you found them
in a closet you haven't touched in years.
The world owes you this, this one perfect thing.

Trade your body for a silent room, flattened by faces

-after a line by Tony Mancus

I took my body to the flea market, but I was
too cheap to pay for a stall. So I stood near
the door. Forgotten housewives careened around
me with terrified faces, until the stallholders signed
a petition that told me to move out of the way.
"I know my rights," we all said at the same time.
I took my body over by the bathroom, hoping
for an impulse buy. I got a few sneers, a few hushed
starers. "Only used once," I said. "Free to a good
home." I rattled off every cliché I could think of.
I've never been good at sales. "Cooks and cleans.
Plenty of room for a new brain." I knocked
on my head, but nobody was looking. It wasn't
much of a body, to be honest. Too much in some
places and not enough in others. "It smells like new
car and has a mostly full set of teeth." I went over
to a donut stall, thinking I'd be better off there,
but most of the customers seemed satisfied
with their creaking knees. "Tastes like new."
An old woman eyed me lasciviously. "How much
for the hair?" she asked. "It's a package deal,"
I said. She cackled like we'd shared a joke.
Someone was tuning a triangle somewhere
behind me. There was a Goodwill down the street.
I didn't think I'd have any better luck there.

Watching *X-Files* in the Dark with You

My feet were still bleeding from the dodo
egg shards when you told me you loved me.
That's the way I learned to spell loss.
I miss my best friend. I don't care how boring
it is to care. No one sees the petard until
they're in the air. Let me stay up there
forever or let me die when I land. This
getting up and walking away business
is filing for Chapter 11. Refurbish my plans
and sell them at a steep discount. You still
have my boxed set. It was the day I moved
out, my soon-to-be ex-wife across town.
Planets spin away, and you'd better be on
the right one. Or you can never go back.
So many times, I haven't believed my eyes.
You are the truth, and you're still out there.

When We Lived On the Sun, We Wore Different Shoes

When I'm feeling nauseous, like after
meals or before having to see people,
I climb on the roof of the nearest building
I can find that reminds me of my father's
house and scream at the sky to fucking
remember my birthday, just once.
I don't expect much, but it would be nice
to be hit by a shooting star before I die.
Maybe with a check for twenty bucks
inside. But it's just more light, looking
for cracks to slip through. The idea
that loneliness has a name. That stillness
exists. When everyone remembers that hate
cannot be contained indefinitely, that it
can grow legs and lumber away from
the couch, this would be a nice place to plant
some corn. Natural light. Retractable ladders.
Block everything off and wait for the smell
to die down. Call it a retirement plan.
Back before, when we didn't know enough
to be upset, we'd stare and stare, thinking—
if we thought at all—that it's tomorrow's
problem, not being able to see.

We Both Know We're Not Getting Out Alive

The moment you've reached the tusk
and are sure it's an elephant, the ground
shifts and you realize you've been floating

all along. What did you think was going
to happen? You've got one flickering bar,
which is barely enough to play Bear Thief,

and you're so close to breaking the top 10.
That will show that kid in Ohio who's
the loser. A person has to have priorities.

You keep poking the thing's eye and wonder
why the universe doesn't see you. It's a matter
of fear that leads to resignation, the austerity

of the universe's resources, overscheduling
of staff meetings. Everything has a way
of grinding to a halt if you give it enough

lead time. Usually, the problem is having
to wait until the motion sickness passes before
you can climb up on its back. Up there, they

say, you can see all the way home. Or at least
back to the ranger station. It's not far from there,
to your car, you're pretty sure. Maybe you

could ask someone. Maybe the elephant knows.

Last Train to Dubuque

I will learn how to shush the flames
with a blink. This is the advantage
of long eyelashes. I will learn
the language of the dust, which mostly
involves controlled sneezing. It isn't
a question of discipline so much as
a cozy proximity with hopelessness.
We've always known the world was
ending, it was just a question of whether
we'd get out of Dubuque before
the rains came. Another six months.
Another eight months. Another thirty
years and I'm definitely done with
this. I've been training myself not
to notice the failures of the world.
First, teach the wind how to properly
pronounce your name. Then, ask it
to never mention you again. I never
needed to write any of this disdain
down; I came by it honest. What I
would really like, right now, is a one-
way ticket to the train station, and then
a map of all the lines. Then, I'll take
it home and think a long time about
places I'm too afraid to ever go.

The sweetened breath of the starving.

-after a line by Dean Young

The truth about the 1% isn't
what we've read in the mandatory
appreciation class. They rarely
spill their seed on the ground,
but when they do, only the cheapest
pines grow. Most do keep a person
of a similar height, weight,
and mimicking dental history in
a comfortable cell basting themselves
with gasoline, to be used as
a body double when we come
with the guillotines. They call
that person Me, regardless of birth
name. In fact, most don't know
its birth name. The rich subsist
on a diet of tobacco smoke enemas
and dolmas stuffed with the sautéed
hearts of any who annoyed them.
Sometimes, they have avocado toast
and then immediately mock millennials.
48% of their pets are androids,
indistinguishable from the real thing.
Of course, an actual animal was
tortured to create the synthetic one.
They watch our lives through hidden
cameras, but grow bored easily
and remove women's healthcare rights,
minority voting access, any illusion

of class progression for ratings purposes.
Upon reaching maturity, each 1%er
is given a jar full of the miracles
meant for starving children in 3rd
world countries but intercepted
by Elon Musk using the latest means.
They are not human, but they've read
the books. Most spend years perfecting
a disaffected slouch to be used
if ever they're caught in the dirty
world of the living. Their natural
language is the complaint. They see
the world, and they want it in chains.

A Yelp Review of Life

3 stars. It was good to be alive, not
as good as we'd hoped or expected.
We supposed that must be our
faults, all evidence to the contrary.
We heard such good things, and some
bad. We did some things, though all
of us ran out pretty early on and struggled
to fill the hours in a way others
respected. A few would've liked to feel
the rotting, the being nibbled
away, but that's probably hind-
sight. For most of it, there wasn't
too much or too little. It was
just enough. But it would've
been nice not to be so stuck
in our heads the whole time.

The Flying Children Tell Their Story

They said that when we found
our wings, we lured our parents
into the woods to kill them. But

it was they who lured us, after first
emptying their quivers into the sky
to knock us down. When we took

to the air, it's true we never came
down, but that's because the hail
of arrows, spears, not to mention

the hateful words they threw at us
made us fear for our meager health.
Our parents cursed us for their own

lives, dying in the mud while we
perched on the treetops. They never
tried to climb up to play in the wind

with us, only to try to drag us back
down. What would you do if one
morning, you woke, your back spread

into feathers? You call to a mother,
a father who never succored you,
and find them jealous. You, your

sister, your brother, all take
to the air to escape the cruelty.
You would fly as far away from

the flat-footed apes as you could,
and no matter how the wind changed,
you wouldn't come back.

The Miracle

I'm tired of waiting for the miracle
to come, so from now on, I'll be waiting
for the science to drop. After a few drinks,
it mostly devolves into discussions
of deviant sex acts. The same could be said
of most situations. Try not to be disappointed
that the sky doesn't look like you, no matter
how blue you feel. It's the ocean reflecting
the sky reflecting how you ache. The sun
runs right through, and you discover there's
nothing there but a little water vapor and good
intentions. Someone is always building
something out of wood next door, but none
of them notice the smoke on the horizon.
If they did, they'd just hammer louder. History
has yet to prove me wrong. Never forget
that your neighbors would sell you to the flames
for the sake of convenience, for the favors
of an imaginary god of paper, for whoever
offers first with the toothiest smile. I know.
It seems like we've come so far, but most
of it was by plane, and none of us know how
to land. No wonder we don't know how
to dress for the weather anymore; it's been
so long since we've seen it truly rain.

The Sun

You can blame me for deflowering
the sun again, again, again, but Ann,
it was a consensual relationship.
We met on a warm fall day. She
had slipped on a light dress which
still showed the shape of her legs.
White, sheer, a nothing that cost
not enough for what it did. Beauty
is always a startling emotion.
The harshest indictment I can stand
is that I'm only a man. Again, again,
again. She lay in the leaves, a spiral
of dying flowers pin-wheeling her head.
Sniffling in the breeze because of all
the damned ornamental trees. What
to say when you can't speak? As foolish
as I sound, that's all I am. The trees
were dropping down their hearts
for the long death ahead. I thought
mine was already gone, but the sap
woke within it, fool that it was. There
were milkshakes. Honey and hubris.
Badly tuned songs and not enough
hands. Too short, and I lost her. Ann,
will you marry me? The sun
is gone. She's not coming back.

The Ghost Nebula

This fucking guy. All right, I'm walking through a corn field—because I was on acid, okay? I don't usually do shit like that. But it was nice, you know, the way the what-do-you-call-them, the leaves or whatever, they sort of rustled in the wind and they brushed against me as I walked, and it had just rained, so it was like running through a field of tongues. Which sounds better when you're on acid. So I see this light in the sky, and I think it's probably John Denver, so I go to it to see if he'll take me to Tennessee, but it's not John Denver. Or, at least I don't think so, I've never met the guy. It's this little gray dude. He tells me his name is Klorax, and I tell him that's not how you spell that. He says he's from this other planet and he's on vacation and wants to hang out. Like I say, I'm on acid, so I say sure and ask him if he knows John Denver. He does not. "Buddy, have I got a treat for you," I say. Then he follows me home, which takes a while, because I can't remember how to use my legs, and I'm afraid to open my eyes because that's how the demons get in and I don't want them to steal all of my toast. So we finally get home, and the guy—the alien—plops right on my couch. Starts watching *Call the Midwife*, which, don't get me wrong. I passed out in my bathtub some time after that, and when I woke up, he was still there. That was three days ago. Turns out, days last 265 years where he's from, and his vacation is a week. And the guy is such a pig, I mean, really. He ate all my Cheez-Its and then says currency is an illusion. He broke my favorite mug and then said mugs are an illusion. The guy ate my remote and the channel changes every time he burps. I miss the tongues. I miss John Denver. That's the last time I buy acid in Nebraska.

Mom Was a Tropical Frozen Drink

Melt for everything or you'll stick
that way, my mother always warned
me. I was little more than a popsicle
stick to her, sweet juice long spent,
splintering on a sidewalk somewhere.
I'd hear her heel click before I saw
her when she came to visit. Then
the tang of coconut and mango.
She'd managed to keep herself
sweet. Maybe it was guilt set her
going like a blender stirring her
fruit, though there was only a
semblance of her in me, and that,
more of a stain on the wood. Once,
I remember a squirrel got ahold of me,
gnawing and chittering. It carried
me to its nest, buried me in acorns
and French fries it'd dug from the trash.
It was comforting to know I was finally
wanted. I lay in the dark bliss of the leaf
ball, cracks letting in light like stars.
Until mom's click clack of plastic on
wood shattered the silence. The squirrel
was out gathering or screwing. I had
no way to fight her. She whisked me
back to the sidewalk. "My little stick,"
she said as I clattered to the bitter concrete.
I knew I'd stay there until she forgot about
me. Someone would have to find her

unsipped essence, suck her into themselves.
If I wasn't dry, I would've cried for my
sad little self. Melt for everything, she
said. But there was nothing left of me
but her.

A Lovely Shade of Purple

This is not the time for me to count thumbs
and wonder who to report to, or how to format
the results. This is the time to cower in the nearest
chicken coop and wait for the fox like a goddamned
American. A slick enough sheet can pass for
an eggshell if you don't have time for papier mache.
Hay is abundant to cower in. You can learn to live
with the itch. Wait in there through the night, singing
a selection of Top 40 Hits from yesteryear. The foxes
get hungriest in the dark. If it hasn't come by morning,
you are not a winner. Please play again and try
to move past the shame of not being eaten. For
the purposes of historical accuracy, how would
you rate your experiences with this Armageddon?
On a scale of 1 to 5, whereas 1 is screaming
oblivion and 5 is the same but someone is poking
you in the side the whole time and trying to ask
you a question about process until your side
becomes a lovely shade of purple and you forget
any complaints you might've had about the
accommodations, answer the following: if God
exists, one can't help but wonder why he doesn't
attend therapy. Holding on to the hate he must have
for us has got to do a number on his digestive system,
his sleep schedule, interpersonal relationships.
We are all in danger of waking up and realizing
there's nothing for us here. The question we all
know the answer to is where should we go next?
I hear Burbank is nice this time of year. But I've
never been there.

The Weight

Grief slides on like an old sweatshirt
from the back of the closet. It smells
like you, fits the curves you wish you

didn't have. This is where you spent
your best days. It's torn in places you
are torn, where the world's claws flicked

through and buried themselves in your
flesh. This sweatshirt is deceptively thick—
it convinces you it will keep you warm,

safe, its weight—lined with dark flowers
maybe no one else has ever seen—slowly
arching your back each day. You think

you'll only wear it until you're dry,
but this is who you are, now. Forgive
someone each day until you work up

the list to yourself. We both know, you'll
never get there, but sometimes, the important
thing is to keep the blood moving.

Dinner Time

Loss stomps in, flops its ax onto
the table top by the door, shattering
it into wood shards, spewing bills

and unread books into the hallway
outside my apartment. I want to have
a conversation about the skull found

in Africa, somewhere, I think.
It belonged to a child, had great talon
holes in its pate. How must its parents

have felt, if they saw her carried
into the sky. Loss has set himself up
on my couch, boots thudded onto

the table we set plates on when we
watch TV instead of speaking during
meals. "I don't care about history,"

Loss says. "But all you care about
is history," I say. Loss doesn't answer.
Instead, he snaps my remote in half,

stares at it like a confused toddler,
unlaces a boot, and throws it at the screen
before I can stop him. "Why are you

here?" I ask. He shrugs. The timer
is going off on the oven. A neighbor
stands outside her doorway, aghast

at the mess in the hall. I'm afraid
to take my eyes off Loss for fear
it will take away something else.

The Flowers

It was high noon when the flowers came.
Blown in from the ocean, we figured,
never questioning why now. They'd come
from some kind of seaweed or sea plant,
is what the radio said. None of us much
listened to the radio anymore, though.

At first, we thought it was pretty. They
were mostly white, big wide petals
like open mouths with some green in
the center. A fly landed in one and it
closed tight. A moment later, the petals
opened and the fly was gone. I remember
somebody applauding. It was a lunch break.

They got bigger. A bird touched one, still
in the air, and it closed around it, nothing
left but a squawk. When it landed, there
wasn't even a feather left. But the flower
seemed bigger. And whiter. Prettier.

I heard stories of someone sticking their nose
in a flower to sniff it, and it closing around
their face. I worried about children and pets.
Through the glass, I could see them flying,
thicker and thicker, larger, settling on top
of cars, in streets, the parking lot, full of them.

By the time I left for the day, the flowers
had grown big enough to eat a person. I
stood in the doorway, watching them blow
past, settling slowly out of the air. There were
fewer of them, now. I had an umbrella in my
desk. I waited an hour and they hadn't stopped
coming, so I opened the umbrella and ran.

The petals curved up at the edge. I could ease
the closed umbrella under and trigger it
to close, long enough to get by. There was one
on top of my car. I ducked beneath it and drove
home. Semis and busses barreled over them.
The roads were mostly clear. I was afraid
to run over any flowers bigger than a car tire. It took
me two hours to make a half-hour drive.

The next morning, I opened my blinds to find
a world of white. There were flowers everywhere.
I could see thin paths between them. I called
the office to see if anyone else was coming in.
The phone rang and rang. Not even Bob answered.
I hoped everyone but Susan was okay.

How To Slay the Dragon

The first question to ask is who
is getting paid for the corpse?
Follow the smell past the wagon
tender, the horse, the undertaker,
the coal seller who stokes the oven.
Another man has paid them all.
Examine the dragon's middle school
report cards, paying special attention
to the home room teachers' narratives
about its behavior, questions of sharing
and respect for others' bodies. Read
the shitty poetry it wrote as a teenager,
notes passed in study hall to scoffing
peers. Email its first boss, but don't
expect a reply. Track down a coworker
to learn about its cleaning skills,
whether it did its part or abandoned
responsibility to others. Compile
a brief list of first date destinations:
homecoming, movie theaters, restaurants,
back alleys. Was it married? If not,
did it travel? If so, track down
the garbage men who sorted out empty
vodka bottles from its trash. Xerox a copy
of the cave's lease, which it took
out after the divorce. Sneak inside
and steal small bits of treasure until
you're able to spread them out and lie
on top. Close your eyes and breathe
its smell in. Now, you are ready to begin.

Marrying the Storm

The wind likes to tell me I'm so weak,
it could kick my ass. It laughed
in my face and said water had more
muscle tone. I've got nothing on stone.
I said, "You don't get to speak to me
like that, now that we're no longer dating."
The wind gave me an old-fashioned look,
the kind that spoke without breath. I wanted
to tell it how much I missed feeling
it flow over me, the little nudge it
sometimes gave me, right in the small
of my back. The wind is stronger than
us all. You may not realize. Try wearing
down a mountain some time. Try
pushing a blade of straw through a tree.
I can't even carry a cow, much less spin
it through the air. "I never loved you,"
it said. "All of it was a mistake." "That's
not true, or you wouldn't feel the need
to say it," I said. "Why are you even
here?" The wind was getting pissed.
"It's not too late," I said. "If you could just
do a little work on yourself. Learn to
communicate better. I could help you,"
I said. "We could see a professional."
The wind scoffed in that dismissive way
I hated. "I don't change for anyone,"
I said. "You change all the time," I said.
It was getting black out. Windows rattled.

Trees danced. "I know you miss us,"
I said. It was calm where I sat. Violence
surrounded me, but I was safe in the eye.

We Must Tell Our Sons

- after Besmilr Brigham

not to be afraid
the world is not
   a curved mirror
   a fist to the eyes
the chest
   a ladder to look down
   over the rest
No, it's not.

if everything hurts
might as well turn
   toward the light
   the warm

there is a secret born
   inside you
   with you
that grows inside you
   a candle flame
so easy to blow out
meant to be shared
the high winds come
   from everywhere
   from those who've forgotten
   their secrets
   who've let their flames be blown out
   who never knew they had a choice
   who were never given a choice

help them

Magic Death

Your magic is a kind of death
swirling in the air like batons.
I don't mind. I've been trying
to kill this noise for years.
Sing and talk and mug and let
this thing wither in me, choked
from the light by a different
kind of light. Really, it's okay.
These twins, one is a kind
of darkness and the other light.
One hides infinity and the other
is hard to look at. Not much
of a difference, really. (Infinity
is just another word for death.
And squinting is just another
way of smiling.) Let's get
a dog and teach it tricks. Let's
grow a garden in pots on the
balcony. There's probably
a ghost somewhere we could
find if you've got comfortable
shoes. If not, let's stop by the store.
I started writing down your jokes
to sell to magazines. Someone
should remember what it was like.
Pick a recipe and we'll make cookies.
I've been saving these ingredients
for years. Vacuum sealed. Wipe
off the dust. Maybe you'll remember

this place, the one that had mice,
the one where everyone treated you
like a superstar. Or maybe you'll
remember that, if you want cookies,
you just have to go make them.
I know you're going to leave me
someday. It's what I've been
teaching you all this time.

You Can Never Go Home Again, Even if You Find the Key

This is what breaks you: waiting
on your father's doorstep for no
one to hear your knock. But at least
you're not on your father's broken
couch, the television screaming over
your better thoughts. This is what
you wanted—to be a stranger
in a life you're holding until someone
comes back for it. Only, you'd hoped
to like it a little more. Not to lord it over
them but just to feel safe. Last time
you were here, you told your father
the trees were all dying in the pasture,
and he said he was doing his best. What
you meant was it's not his fault branches
fall in the yard. We all hope to be missed
more, even the blossoms hitching rides
on the wind. Down the hill, water stagnates
over your old tennis shoe, fishing poles,
long-forgotten toys. The 100-year mud
once almost swallowed you, but now has
forgotten your name. The track up
from the shore is overgrown with bitterweeds.
Sometimes, life has a sense of humor.
Where you are, now, you'll never return
from. There's nothing left of the weight
you once pressed on this soil. The greatest
comfort, you'll come to realize, is in that
forgetting, and being forgotten.

Also By CL Bledsoe

Poetry:

______(Want/Need)
Anthem
Leap Year
Riceland
Trashcans in Love
King of Loneliness
I Never Promised You a Sea Monkey (with Michael Gushue)
Give me
Grief Bacon
Driving Around, Looking in Other People's Windows

Fiction:

Naming the Animals, Collected Stories
Sunlight
The Necro-Files: $7.50/Hr + Curses
The Necro-Files: Bloody Sexy
The Necro-Files: Tall, Dark, & Hairy
Last Stand In Zombietown
Sorting the Dead
Man of Clay
Ray's Sea World, Collected Flash Stories
The Funny Thing About...
The Show Fixture Played the Blues, Collected Stories
Goodbye Mr. Lonely
The Saviors